How My Body Moves

by Ulrik Hvass

Illustrated by Volker Theinhardt

VIKING KESTREL

Take a pair of jeans by the waistband and hold them upright. What happens when you let go?

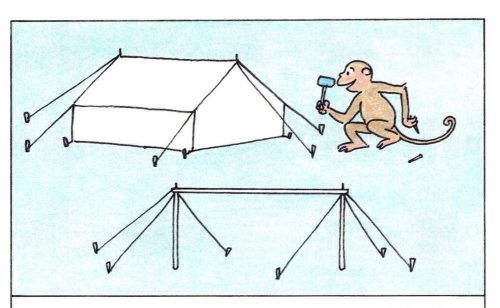

If you take the canvas off a tent, you can see the frame which makes the tent stay upright. If you took this frame away, then the canvas would fall down just like the jeans did. The frame makes the tent stand upright, but it doesn't make the tent able to move around by itself.

If you feel along your arm or leg, you'll feel something hard inside. That's your bones! You have lots of bones inside your body. Many are like stiff tubes. Some are long, like the bones in your arms and legs. Some bones are short, as in your fingers and toes. All your bones together form your skeleton.

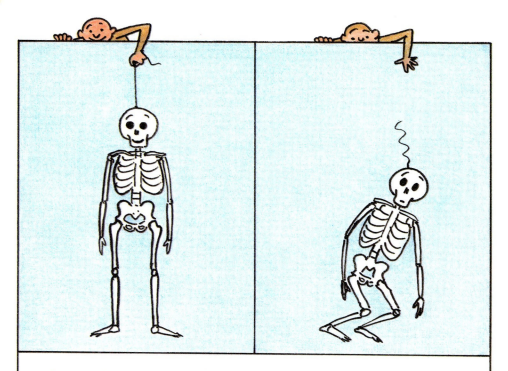

But a skeleton can't stand up on its own. If one is held upright and then let go of, it just falls down.

So how do you stand up and move around on your own?

Lie down on the ground. Then slowly sit up. Watch carefully how your body moves and feel what effort it takes.

Now look at this wooden puppet. Its elbows and knees bend. The two pieces of wood that form each leg are linked together at the knee. The bones in your legs are also linked together at the knee in a similar way. The place where two bones are linked and where they are thus able to move is called a joint.

You can make a model of a joint to see how it works. You'll need two pieces of wood, some tape, a rubber band, and two drawing pins. Join the two pieces of wood with the tape.

Use the two drawing pins to fix the rubber band on one of the pieces of wood. Hold the wood down with your finger and pull on the rubber band. Nothing happens to the other piece of wood.

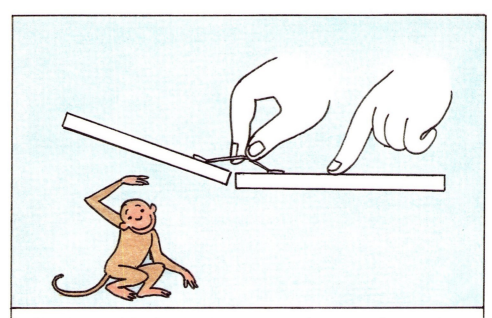

Now fix the rubber band to the two pieces of wood, as shown in the picture. Hold down one of the pieces of wood with your finger and pull on the rubber band. The other piece of wood moves at the place where the two pieces are joined.

What is the force that moves your joints? You can feel your muscles under your skin. They work rather like the rubber band. They're stretchy and can lengthen or shorten themselves.

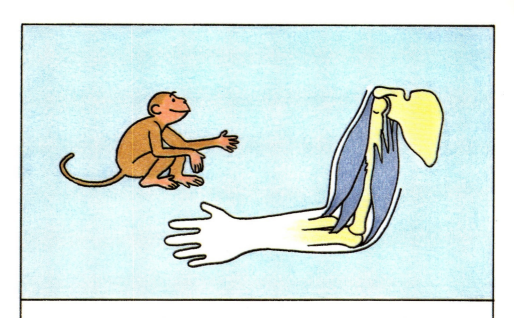

Your muscles are fixed onto both sides of your joints, and they control the movement of the bones. The part of the muscle that is wrapped around the joint is often much thinner than the rest of the muscle. This part is called a tendon.

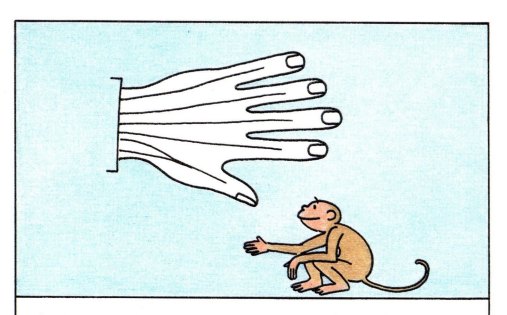

Look at the back of your hand and wiggle your fingers. You can see lots of tendons moving. Your fingers move like the joints of a puppet on a string. Try to find other tendons—look at your knees, heels, and feet.

If you bend your arms and legs, you are able to straighten them again. If you couldn't, your arms and legs would stay bent! Each joint has a second set of muscles which control movement in the opposite direction.

Working together, the bones that make up your skeleton, the joints, groups of muscles, and tendons all enable your body to move.
But who tells your muscles to move?

You do! You tell them what you want to do and they obey you. You're so used to doing this that you can do most movements without thinking.

But you'll find that it takes time for your muscles to learn a new movement. Try to move your fingers as shown in the picture.

Where does the order "Muscles, make me stand up!" come from? It comes from your brain.

But how can your brain do that when it's so far away from your muscles?

Here's an easy experiment to show how remote control works. Take a bulb and touch both terminals of a battery with the base. The bulb lights up. When you take the bulb away from the battery, the light goes out. Now use long electric wires to connect the battery and the bulb. The bulb lights up again.

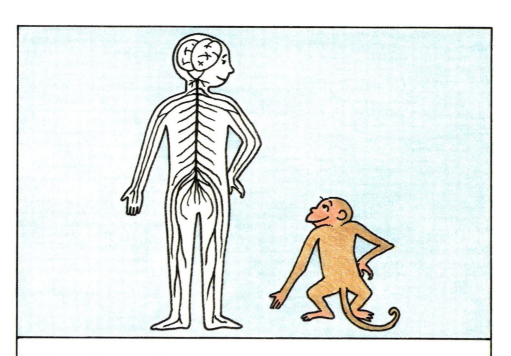

A special system of wires, or nerves, connects your brain with all the muscles in your body.

There are some illnesses that stop people from being able to move properly. Polio is one of these illnesses. It destroys some of the nerves, which means that commands from the brain can't reach all the muscles. Polio used to be quite a common illness, but nowadays, fortunately, vaccination prevents it.

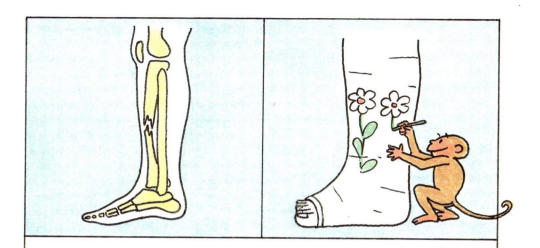

Sometimes a bone is broken in an accident. That's called a fracture. For a bone to heal properly it must be kept still. A plaster cast will stop the joints on either side of the fracture from moving. When the plaster is taken off, it will take some time before the leg can move as it did before because the leg will be stiff from being kept still so long.

To be able to move you need:
—a skeleton with its joints
—muscles to make your skeleton move
—a brain to command your muscles
—and nerves to bring the command from your brain to your muscles.

VIKING KESTREL
Viking Penguin Inc., 40 West 23rd Street, New York, New York 10010, U.S.A.
Penguin Books Ltd, Harmondsworth, Middlesex, England
Penguin Books Australia Ltd, Ringwood, Victoria, Australia
Penguin Books Canada Limited, 2801 John Street, Markham, Ontario, Canada L3R 1B4
Penguin Books (N.Z.) Ltd, 182-190 Wairau Road, Auckland 10, New Zealand

Translation copyright © Éditions du Centurion, Paris, 1986
All rights reserved

First published in France as *Les Mouvements du corps* by
Éditions du Centurion, 1986. © 1986, Éditions du Centurion, Paris.
This English-language edition first published in 1986 by Viking Penguin Inc.
Published simultaneously in Canada
Printed in France by Offset Aubin, Poitiers
1 2 3 4 5 90 89 88 87 86

Library of Congress catalog card number: 86-40007
(CIP data available)
ISBN 0-670-81199-8

Without limiting the rights under copyright reserved above, no part of this
publication may be reproduced, stored in or introduced into a retrieval system,
or transmitted, in any form or by any means (electronic, mechanical, photocopying,
recording or otherwise), without the prior written permission of both the
copyright owner and the above publisher of this book.